# Overcoming Loss

*of related interest*

**Talking with Children and Young People about Death and Dying**
**Second Edition**
*Mary Turner*
Illustrated by Bob Thomas
ISBN 978 1 84310 516 9

**Grief in Children**
**A Handbook for Adults**
**Second Edition**
*Atle Dyregrov*
ISBN 978 1 84310 612 8

**Grief in Young Children**
**A Handbook for Adults**
*Atle Dyregrov*
ISBN 978 1 84310 650 0

**The Colors of Grief**
**Understanding a Child's Journey through Loss from Birth to Adulthood**
*Janis A. Di Ciacco*
ISBN 978 1 84310 886 3

**Empowering Children through Art and Expression**
**Culturally Sensitive Ways of Healing Trauma and Grief**
*Bruce St Thomas and Paul Johnson*
ISBN 978 1 84310 789 7

**Grandad's Ashes**
*Walter Smith*
ISBN 978 1 84310 517 6

**When a Family Pet Dies**
**A Guide to Dealing with Children's Loss**
*JoAnn Tuzeo-Jarolmen, Ph.D.*
ISBN 978 1 84310 836 8

# Overcoming Loss

**Activities** and **Stories**
to Help Transform **Children's**
**Grief** and **Loss**

## Julia Sorensen

Illustrated by Maryam Ahmad

Jessica Kingsley Publishers
London and Philadelphia

First published in 2008
by Jessica Kingsley Publishers
116 Pentonville Road
London N1 9JB, UK
and
400 Market Street, Suite 400
Philadelphia, PA 19106, USA

*www.jkp.com*

Copyright © Julia Sorensen 2008
Illustrations Copyright © Maryam Ahmad 2008

**Library of Congress Cataloging in Publication Data**
Sorensen, Julia.
  Overcoming loss : activities and stories to help transform children's grief and loss / Julia Sorensen.
    p. cm.
  ISBN 978-1-84310-646-3 (alk. paper)
  1.  Grief in children. 2.  Bereavement in children. 3.  Loss (Psychology) in children.  I. Title.
  BF723.G75S67 2008
  155.9'3083--dc22

                              2007052367


**British Library Cataloguing in Publication Data**
A CIP catalogue record for this book is available from the British Library

ISBN 978 1 84310 646 3


Printed and bound in Great Britain by
Athenaeum Press, Gateshead, Tyne and Wear

*This book is dedicated to
my daughter Hannah*

# Contents

# Introduction

This book was written for children and the adults who help them discover healing ways to express their own unique personalities. The book draws on, and integrates, the best of approaches: social emotional learning, emotional EQ, Developmental Approaches, Expressive Therapy and Cognitive Behavioral Therapy. Its focus is to bring expressive and transformational experiences to the child as they strive to overcome their losses.

When helping children identify their problems, it is often difficult to find resources that are accurate and simple. A starting-off point would be to be able to identify the problem, discover a workable plan for overcoming the difficulty, and bringing about resolution to the problem.

However, when collaborating with parents, schools, and communities, it may be better to provide resources that can help children understand *what* their feelings are and then help them express *what* those emotions are. As adults we often expect children to understand strong feelings such as *anger, sadness, jealousy, frustration*, but those emotions are more comfortably communicated through their play, or art work.

This book is transformational because it:

- helps the child to understand and express strong feelings

- normalizes the child and adult about the strong feelings toward losses

- provides a foundation for children to work through painful experiences and then to discover new ways to perceive those experiences in their thinking styles

- it helps young people lay the groundwork for Cognitive Behavioral Therapy (CBT) by generating as many new explanations or alternative perspectives about a situation as possible. This is accomplished by helping children to brainstorm new thinking patterns. Children can be assisted to do this through discovering new ways to play, to remember, to express the closure, and to think about themselves

- creates a starting-off point for discussion and creative expression through written words, drawing, and stories

- helps the child build a vocabulary of feeling words and develops emotional literacy

- enables the child to shift their perception from one of loss to the resolving of their grief over time.

# How to use this workbook

## Why this book was written

This book was written to help children and the adults that work with them to access a simple resource. It provides a foundation for children to express their sadness, anger, and loss at giving closure to a relationship through death, trauma, multiple losses, through moving to another community, through divorce, separation, or other endings.

Parents and professionals are often confused about how to help children understand or express their feelings. Children often don't know *what* they are feeling except a vague sense of confusion and discomfort which is more likely to be expressed through play, or through behavioral difficulties. To help these children move closer to expressing their feelings and resolving those feelings means that we need to equip them with the words and materials to process their endings.

## What you will see

This book is laid out in four separate parts. Each part can be worked through individually from beginning to end, or, it may be used in individual ways, for example starting at Part III, which is a short story about multiple losses experienced by a young skink (from the lizard family).

## How to look at the exercises

The workbook begins by suggesting that the child is made to feel comfortable and safe. The exercises start by making a list of feeling words, which help the child to recognize facial expressions, to act and write feeling words, to learn the "color" of the feelings they experience, and to integrate this learning.

The second part socializes the child to loss experiences and the stages of normal sadness after a loss, whether from a divorce, a move, or death of a loved one or a pet. This section focuses on creating a positive memory and a way to honor the memory.

The third section is a short story about a little lizard whose family had to fight to survive in nature. The fictional story's character, "Lilly", experiences several losses from natural disasters which lead to her experience overwhelming emotions that she thinks will never go away.

Over time, and with the support of her dear grandmother, Lilly is able to create a good place to remember her missed ones and a place where she can come to remember them. Lilly learns that her strong feelings subside and she starts to experience joy and happiness in her life as she resumes a normal routine that any youngster might enjoy.

There is no right or wrong way to view the art and exercises of a child. The helper is there to facilitate their creative expressions of closure without judgment.

The stages of grief are *shock*, *denial*, *anger*, *bargaining*, *sadness*, and *acceptance* with children following their own path to closure in very different ways. Some of these ways help the child express and accept the reality of the loss, experience the pain of the loss, adjust to a new reality without the loss, and, finally, to establish a new identity without the loss.

Some children will travel through all the stages in a consistent manner; some will miss stages or regress backwards for a while, some may outwardly appear to be unaffected by the loss but emotionally may be experiencing considerable pain. Rather like adults, there is no right or wrong way for children to resolve feelings. They simply need to be encouraged to feel and accept their own feelings, both negative and positive, at the time they are expressing them. Caregivers can ensure that children keep normal routines as this provides safety for them. The Resources section also provides further information and handouts for the reader.

If there are signals that a child is stuck, say in the anger stage for a long period of time, seek professional consultation from a counselor or psychologist. Play and expressive art work can be beneficial in enabling the child to express their pain and, ultimately, to transform it.

# Part I:
# Expressive activities

*Feelings*

**Activity 1**   Creating a safe place to be…: An introduction to feeling work

**Activity 2**   Feeling puzzle: What are the names of your feelings?

**Activity 3**   Match the feeling game: Recognizing your feelings

**Activity 4**   Faces collage: Learning what emotions are expressed on faces

**Activity 5**   Feeling faces: Draw a face to match the feeling word

**Activity 6**   Feeling words: Building a vocabulary of feeling words

**Activity 7**   Finish the sentence…: Choose a feeling word from the vocabulary list to end these sentences

**Activity 8**   What color are my feelings?: Find out what color your feelings are

**Activity 9**   Feelings rainbow: Expressing your feelings through colors

# Introduction to expressive activities: Feelings

## Note to readers

The ability to accurately identify and express feelings is a part of social emotional learning (SEL). Children naturally identify with, and express feelings through their play, art, or metaphorical stories. Language and recognition of more subtle emotions does not occur until much later. Children will tend to understand and verbalize the spectrums of feelings: happy, sad, and angry but have little understanding of less intense or moderate feelings.

More subtle emotions such as shame, humiliation, despair, and jealousy are not recognized but are nevertheless felt by children. Expressing such feelings usually occurs through imaginative play, art, or identification with characters in stories.

More difficult-to-label emotions pose a problem for children experiencing loss at any level. Divorce, separation, death, leaving a community, losing a beloved parent's attention through depression, financial stress, a new job, a new sibling arrival, or the loss of a pet are all examples of loss for children, and yet our culture does not honor these losses with ritual or respect.

For children to overcome their feelings of grief, however insignificant they may seem to adults, a vehicle is needed to express that loss through play, through art, and through stories. These simple exercises will help children through the normal stages of loss: disbelief and shock, denial, anger, bargaining, sadness, and acceptance.

Grief stages are a tool for adults to recognize and acknowledge but should not be used as an authoritative guide to determine which stage a child is in. To measure a child's health against these stages and to move them through the stages as quickly as possible would be counterproductive for the child. Children can work from beginning to end, can regress backwards or skip stages and then regress. The work that the child does as they strive for healing is unique to each.

The first exercise looks at creating emotional and environmental safety in which to set the stage to help children feel comfortable in expressing feelings. This exercise encourages children to define and take the lead in finding a space that is comfortable.

Each child is individual and will seek emotional safety in different ways. For some children it will be on the floor, for others in a favorite chair, or outside in a garden sitting underneath a tree, or at a playground. If you allow the child to lead, they will guide you to learn how they define their own feelings of emotional safety.

Setting the stage for emotional or feeling work is an important part of helping the child to feel safe and to allow them to be vulnerable to express difficult emotions later on. Children cannot expect to transform the stages of loss and reintegrate their feelings if they cannot experience these difficult feelings and work through them. Transforming loss is not about skipping stages, denying the feelings that emerge, and having the child get on with their lives. It is rather a ritual of honoring the time and ways that are needed to express such emotions and gain a new perspective on their loss.

Activity 1 accomplishes the primary goal of setting the stage for feeling work. It asks the child to take the lead in determining where the feeling work can take place, and what favorite items and toys the child will need to experience emotional safety.

The writing and drawing activities are included in large font so that children with emerging handwriting and fine motor coordination skills will have plenty of space to express their work. It would also be helpful to have extra paper and drawing materials on hand, such as pencils, crayons, markers, paints, glue, scissors, and old magazines, so that children can utilize both color and favorite medium when working through the exercises.

The exercises are provided on a continuum so that children can transform and resolve their feelings. The initial activities start with setting the stage, and progress to learning about and identifying a wide range of feelings. Once the child has identified feelings, the activities presented help children resolve their own feelings, and their own experiences of closure in small or large ways. The activities then provide an expressive space to draw or write about such experiences. The expression of these activities provides opportunities for children to honor their memories through activities, and finally by identifying with a loss through a short fictional story.

Although the activities are provided on a continuum, they can be proceeded through in different ways, say with the short story after the identification of feelings activities. Some children may wish to perform one activity several times, such as drawing about their own loss times, or later in the book by honoring the loss through ritual for several different losses. This will indicate to the facilitator that these are the areas that are needing to be transformed the most, and extra respect for facilitating closure in these areas can be given.

Activities can be expanded upon by developing your own expressive activities, or by extending the work through the reading of fictional stories about grief. A reading list is provided in the resources section to develop children's sense of closure through fiction.

If at any time you become concerned about the progress of a child's expression of closure, consult with a specialist. Resources are provided for appropriate associations, including web resources, to enable you to locate the best and timely help.

# Activity 1 Creating a safe place to be...:

## An introduction to feeling work

> You may wish to find a safe and cozy place to do this exercise. Perhaps sit on the floor, in your favorite spot, with your best loved toy or a comfortable blanket.

Sometimes it is hard to say goodbye to people, animals, or things. Sometimes the things we feel inside are difficult to talk about out loud.

Talking about difficult feelings is sometimes easier to talk about in a different way like drawing, painting, or playing with a favorite toy.

If this is like you, drawing what is on the inside will help you to feel better on the outside.

# Activity 1 Creating a safe place to be...

Draw below your favorite way to feel happy and safe. What are your favorite toys and people to have around you?

# Activity 2 Feeling puzzle:

## What are the names of your feelings?

### Note to readers

The second activity, the Feeling Puzzle, socializes the child very simply to the names of basic feelings. Adults can assume that children understand and can identify these feeling words but care needs to be taken to lay the foundation for the most basic of feeling words. Once this foundation is established, the more difficult and subtle feeling words can be added to a child's feeling vocabulary.

This exercise works on a continuum from simple to complex names and understanding of emotions. Children often learn to express these basic emotions through music, songs, imaginative play, and reading fictional stories. These basic activities can be extended in such ways.

# Activity 2 Feeling puzzle:

## What are the names of your feelings?

Let's make a list of feeling words to use in our pictures. Here are a few feeling words to get you started:

- I **love** playing with my favorite toys.

- I am **angry** when my ice cream cone falls on the floor.

- I am **happy** when it is my birthday.

- I am **frightened** when I see a picture of a **scary** monster.

- I am **proud** of myself when I learn something new.

- I am **surprised** when a friend comes over to play and I didn't know they were coming.

- I feel **sad** for a minute when Mommy goes to work.

- I feel **lonely** when I wake in the middle of the night.

## See if you can guess what these two faces are feeling?

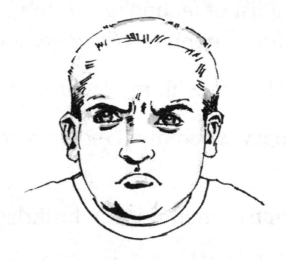

# Activity 3 Match the feeling game:

## Recognizing your feelings

### *Note to readers*

This activity and the one that follows builds on the foundation of Activity 2 by building experientially on identifying the names of feelings and recognizing the emotions that are expressed on the face. Children often have more difficulty due to their age at recognizing the differences between some of the feelings. For example, they may observe a photo or magazine picture of a person demonstrating surprise and label it "fear," or, they may look at a face that demonstrates anger and label it a "frightened face." These subtleties can be alleviated through practice and communication about what emotion the child is observing. Extending the activities by asking them to gesture on their own faces the feeling word can provide additional practice. By matching the vocabulary word to the matching face in Activity 3 will provide practice to develop emotional literacy.

# Activity 3 Match the feeling game:

## Recognizing your feelings

Here are some more faces. See if you can match up the feeling word to the face by drawing a line:

jealous

sad

happy

scared

# Activity 4 Faces collage:

## Learning what emotions are expressed on faces

### *Note to readers*

Activity 4 helps the child to locate all types of facial expressions through magazines and photos to express their own feeling faces. Help the child to identify the themes of the feelings that come out of the collage. Are they mostly happy, sad, frightened, or angry faces that the child has chosen to put in their collage? This will give you a clue as to how they are experiencing their world at that time. Extend the activity through conversation by asking open-ended questions about the emotions you observe in their collage.

# Activity 4 Faces collage:

## Learning what emotions are expressed on faces

Cut or tear as many faces as you can find in magazines and glue in the box below. See if you can guess what each face is feeling. Are they **angry**, **sad**, **jealous**, **happy**, **ashamed**, **frightened**?

# Activity 5 Feeling faces:

## Draw a face to match the feeling word

### Note to readers

This activity asks the child to develop by drawing their own face to match the feeling words. This exercise promotes comprehension of emotions from word to facial gesture. Again, it will provide information to the facilitator about how the child understands what the feeling word is and how it is expressed. Activity 5 acts as a foundation to Activity 6 in which an extended emotional word vocabulary is provided and utilized.

# Activity 5 Feeling faces:

# Draw a face to match the feeling word

*Happy words*

Draw a *face* to match each happy *word*

**joyful**   ┈┈┈┈┈┈┈┈➤

**blissful**   ┈┈┈┈┈┈┈➤

**ecstatic**   ┈┈┈┈┈┈➤

**awesome**   ┈┈┈┈┈➤

**glad**   ┈┈┈┈┈┈➤

# Activity 6 Feeling words

## Building a vocabulary of feeling words

### Note to readers

Activity 6 promotes the development of feeling words and builds vocabulary for four individual emotions: happy, sad, angry, and scared. It provides eight other feeling words under each emotion but there are many more that can be used and utilized through extended activities and reading.

The simple vocabulary list socializes the child to other words beyond happy, sad, angry, and scared. It asks the child to identify and use one other word to describe the same emotion so that feeling words are developed.

# Activity 6 Feeling words:

## Building a vocabulary of feeling words

### Feelings vocabulary

| Happy | Sad | Angry | Scared |
|-------|-----|-------|--------|
| Excited | Hopeless | Furious | Terrified |
| Overjoyed | Sorrowful | Seething | Petrified |
| Elated | Depressed | Enraged | Alarmed |
| Great | Lonely | Fuming | Panicked |
| Ecstatic | Discouraged | Bitter | Fearful |
| Cheerful | Down | Annoyed | Afraid |
| Joyful | Miserable | Frustrated | Anxious |
| Delighted | Low | Irritated | Nervous |

Here are many feeling words. You probably have heard of some of them but some may be new to you. If you look down the columns, you can see that there are many new words for the words: **happy**, **sad**, **angry**, or **scared**.

# Finding a new feeling word

Use the feelings vocabulary list to choose a new word:

## Sad words

**miserable**
**grieving**
**depressed**

Write your sad word here _ _ _ _ _ _ _ _ _ _ _ _ _ _ _ _ _ _ _

## Angry words

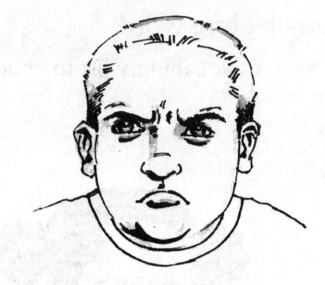

**furious**
**enraged**
**vengeful**

Write your angry word here   _ _ _ _ _ _ _ _ _ _ _ _ _ _ _ _

## *Happy words*

**excited**

**cheerful**

**delighted**

Write your happy word here _ _ _ _ _ _ _ _ _ _ _ _ _ _ _ _ _

## *Scared words*

**frightened**
**terrified**
**afraid**

Write your scared word here _ _ _ _ _ _ _ _ _ _ _ _ _ _ _ _

# Activity 7 Finish the sentence...

## Choose a feeling word from the vocabulary list to end these sentences

### Note to readers

Activity 7 extends the preceding exercise by allowing the child to use their own emotional words to recognize and build emotional literacy. The activity extends beyond the usual happy and sad feelings to help the child to express more difficult and dark emotions.

The child will end the following sentences by choosing a word from the vocabulary list on p.32 and in Appendix B.

# Activity 7 Finish the sentence...:

Choose a feeling word from the vocabulary list to end these sentences:

- When my dog wags his tail at me to say hello, I

  feel _ _ _ _ _ _ _ _ _ _ _ _ _ _ _ _ _ _ _ _ _ _ _ _ _ _ _

- If my friend calls for me to play, I feel  _ _ _ _ _ _

  _ _ _ _ _ _ _ _ _ _ _ _ _ _ _ _ _ _ _ _ _ _ _ _ _ _

- When I have to leave my favorite stuffed toy at home, I might feel _ _ _ _ _ _ _ _ _ _ _ _ _ _ _ _ _ _

- Sometimes a scary cartoon comes on TV and I feel

    _ _ _ _ _ _ _ _ _ _ _ _ _ _ _ _ _ _ _ _ _ _ _

- I was called a mean name by a classmate and I felt _ _ _ _ _ _ _ _ _ _ _ _ _ _ _ _ _ _ _ _ _ _

- Last summer I found a caterpillar and put it in a jar. The next day the caterpillar had crawled out and I felt _ _ _ _ _ _ _ _ _ _ _ _ _ _ _ _ _ _ _ _

- After my grandmother leaves, I feel _ _ _ _ _ _ _ _

    _ _ _ _ _ _ _ _ _ _ _ _ _ _ _ _ _ _ _ _ _ _ _

# Activity 8 What color are my feelings?:

## Find out what color your feelings are

### *Note to readers*

In Activity 8, the child is asked to identify their feelings through color. This exercise allows the child and facilitator to identify what colors are used to express strong emotions through art and drawing. Typically we think of the color red as the color of anger but for the child, red may mean a completely different emotion, such as surprise or excitement. Be careful not to lead the child in what colors they pick. This individualized exercise can lead the facilitator to gather more specific information about the child's expressive work and their need toward healing.

# Activity 8 What color are my feelings?:

## Find out what color your feelings are

| You will need colored pencils, markers, or crayons |

- When I feel **angry**, this is the color of my anger ☐

- When I feel **hurt**, this is the color of my hurt ☐

- When I feel **sad**, this is the color of my sadness ☐

- When I feel **happy**, this is the color of my happiness ☐

- When I feel **jealous**, this is the color of my jealousy ☐

- When I feel **frustrated**, this is the color of my frustration ☐

- When I feel **scared**, this is the color of my fear ☐

# Activity 9 Feelings rainbow:

## Expressing your feelings through colors

### Note to readers

Activity 9 integrates earlier learning by developing individualized feeling colors which will later be developed by drawing a rainbow. This exercise combines a feeling word with a color. Children will choose different and individualized colors to represent strong feelings such as anger or sadness. These colors may be different from the ones we have learned to associate feelings with, such as red for anger. By drawing a rainbow, the child can use the color palette developed in Activity 8 to complete the colors in the rainbow in Activity 9. This way, a symbolic color is chosen to represent each emotion and transferred into the drawing of the rainbow.

For example, one ray may be shaded pink because this is the color chosen to represent angry feelings in Activity 8. Another ray may be colored green which may have been chosen to represent happy feelings in Activity 8. Complete the rainbow with 7 different rays, each one representing an emotion from Activity 7.

# Activity 9 Feelings rainbow:

## Expressing your feelings through colors

Together we can make a rainbow of colors and name each one of the bands a feeling.

You will need crayons, colored pencils, or markers

Draw a rainbow in the box on the next page and color each band with one of the feeling colors you chose for the last exercise.

For example, if you colored the feeling of *anger* an orange color, then color one of your rays orange.

# Draw as many rainbows as you like:

# Part II:
# Expressive activities

*Identifying everyday losses*

**Activity 10** Saying goodbye is hard to do: Learning about everyday closures

**Activity 11** Talking about losses of pets or toys: Recognizing, talking about, and drawing pet or toy losses

**Activity 12** Good memories: Gathering memories

**Activity 13** Memory boxes: A place to honor

**Activity 14** New perspectives: A new way to remember and feel

# Activity 10 Saying goodbye is hard to do:

## Learning about everyday closures

### Note to readers

All children and adults experience everyday closures and endings but because we are so used to them, they become part of the normal repertoire of our days. Some of the closings to our day include saying goodbye to children on our way to work. Another is saying goodbye to colleagues at the end of the work day.

For children, these closures include saying goodbye to parents when leaving for school or day care, and to caregivers at the end of the day when parents pick them up. All of these transitions are endings and beginnings on a subtle, unacknowledged level.

Children experience such closing when grandparents leave to go home after a visit, when parents divorce, families become estranged, or move communities. There are many, many ways that relationships that have been formed through everyday connections become unconnected, presenting children and families with closure.

This exercise socializes the child to the simple, everyday closures they may experience and to the understanding that, even in the beginning, saying goodbye to parents, caregivers, friends, and loved ones is hard to do but it eventually becomes easier, and even an enjoyable experience, as the child reintegrates back into normal routines.

# Activity 10 Saying goodbye is hard to do:

## Learning about everyday closures

Have you ever had to say goodbye to someone you cared about in your life? You probably found it hard to do, especially if you had good and happy feelings about the person.

Every day we say goodbye to many people, perhaps your mom when she goes to work, perhaps a grandparent who returns home after a visit, or, maybe a friend who has to go home after a play date.

Whatever happened, it is likely that you have had both good and bad endings to your day, or to your week.

There may have been times, too, when you were not having such a great time, maybe a bad day at school or when you were on an outing and you could not wait to get home. These were the times when saying goodbye at the end was easier to do.

So you see, some goodbyes are easier than others. Can you think of a time when saying goodbye was hard?

Draw below a time when you had a hard time saying goodbye to someone. Draw as many pictures as you like:

More space for drawing or doodling about your goodbye times:

# Activity 11 Talking about losses of pets or toys:

## Recognizing, talking about, and drawing pet or toy losses

### *Note to readers*

Helping children either experientially or to verbally express the ending or closure can be the vehicle to create new opportunities for further discussion and healing work. This may be a catalyst that enables further work to be initiated by the child.

Activity 11 is a special exercise for pet animal and toy losses, a place to honor and express the loss of a special pet or favorite toy. Losing a favorite or cuddly toy can be a difficult experience for a young child, especially around transitions, goodbyes, or bedtimes. Any caregiver can remember the anguish of trying to locate a beloved toy that has been left at someone's home, on the train, bus or car. This activity, coupled with earlier activities can be utilized to help the child remember the pet or toy. Later exercises, such as making the memory box, can also be used to gather photos and memorabilia of the item.

# Activity 11 Talking about losses of pets or toys:

## Recognizing, talking about, and drawing pet or toy losses

Think about a time when you had a beloved pet, insect, or lost a favorite stuffed toy

What was its name? _____

Draw a picture of your pet below:

# Activity 12 Good memories:

## Gathering memories

### *Note to readers*

The next activities focus on remembering, honoring, and transforming the closure, ending, or loss. These activities respectfully lead the child to gather favorite items belonging to the loved one: to draw, paint, write, or otherwise express in positive ways, the connections made to the person.

In these gentle exercises, the child can be invited to join in their own journey to express the lost relationship. If the facilitator allows the child to set their own pace, they will show the adult who, what, where, and how they are able to process and transform the ending.

These exercises also lead the child to develop a memory and emotional connection with the loss in place of the earlier relationship in physical form. It in essence helps the child to talk about the closure in an open way, it helps facilitate open discussion about the closure and it provides a link from the earlier physical relationship to one that cannot be experienced by physical senses. Children are cognitively very good at this as their imaginations are usually rich and creative in play and expressive work. It is adults who have more difficult times transcending the loss relationship in this way.

# Activity 12 Good memories:

## Gathering memories

> You will need a shoe box, tissue box, or small container to keep your memories in.

Saying goodbye for good doesn't mean that we have to forget the person, animal, or place we left.

For this activity, collect small items such as photos, tickets, keepsakes, pictures you have, or the person you are remembering has drawn. Make a memory list of all activities you did together. Gather anything that will fit into your memory shoe box that is special to you and the person, pet, or place you are remembering.

Remember to go slowly, only do as much as you can handle. It is normal to feel some of those feelings we talked about earlier, like sadness or anger. Or perhaps you feel like a washing machine with all your feelings being tossed around at once—it's ok, we all feel like that sometimes.

It means that we have to work hard to find small ways to remember the people we love and have said goodbye to, and to remember them forever.

# Activity 13 Memory boxes:

## A place to honor

### *Note to readers*

See the 'Note to readers' for Activity 12.

# Activity 13 Memory boxes:

## A place to honor

You may wish to paint, color, or draw on the outside or inside of the container to make it special. You may wish to glue important items on the outside. Do whatever you wish to make it unique to you and the person you are remembering.

When you have completed decorating your shoe box or small container, place all the items that you wish to include inside it gently.

You may wish to line the bottom of it with special paper or material. You may wish to wrap the items before you place them in the container or memory box.

If you don't want to put your memory items in a box or container, you can arrange them on a special shelf.

If you wrap your chosen memories up, remember that you may wish to open them again at a later time and not only add more memories but also to look at the ones you have already placed inside.

When you have added all you that you wish, close your eyes gently and quietly repeat the following sentence:

> I will always remember you. Please take care and know you will always be in my memories.

Now take your container and place it carefully somewhere that is dry and clean, like a bookshelf or in a closet.

Make this place your memory spot and know how to find it when you need to remember the person, animal, or memory again.

# Activity 14 New perspectives:

## A new way to remember and feel

### Note to readers

This exercise acknowledges the transformation and healing work that has taken place with the child. It enables the child to feel safe, emotionally secure and hopeful for the future when generating new perspectives and thinking patterns (Cognitive Behavioral Therapy).

Children are very good at creating many different "stories" about their lives and can be guided to adopt a new perspective for themselves that embraces the healing or closure in an acceptable way. Rather than the child saying, "My friend has moved away," which produces feelings of loss, alternative ideas could be generated by saying, "My best friend lived in my community for two years and has a new community to live in now. We made a memory box and I remember him when I look at it. He is still my friend." This generates thoughts of acceptance and helps to transform the pain of loss to healing.

This exercise can also be used as an evaluation exercise for grief groups.

# Activity 14 New perspectives:

## A new way to remember and feel

Write about or draw below how you are *feeling now* or what feeling *words* you know since you worked through these exercises:

‒ ‒ ‒ ‒ ‒ ‒ ‒ ‒ ‒ ‒ ‒ ‒ ‒ ‒ ‒ ‒ ‒ ‒ ‒ ‒ ‒ ‒ ‒ ‒ ‒ ‒

‒ ‒ ‒ ‒ ‒ ‒ ‒ ‒ ‒ ‒ ‒ ‒ ‒ ‒ ‒ ‒ ‒ ‒ ‒ ‒ ‒ ‒ ‒ ‒ ‒ ‒

‒ ‒ ‒ ‒ ‒ ‒ ‒ ‒ ‒ ‒ ‒ ‒ ‒ ‒ ‒ ‒ ‒ ‒ ‒ ‒ ‒ ‒ ‒ ‒ ‒ ‒

‒ ‒ ‒ ‒ ‒ ‒ ‒ ‒ ‒ ‒ ‒ ‒ ‒ ‒ ‒ ‒ ‒ ‒ ‒ ‒ ‒ ‒ ‒ ‒ ‒ ‒

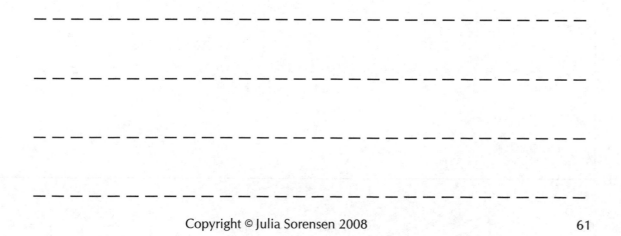

Write about or draw how you are feeling about your goodbye time now:

‒ ‒ ‒ ‒ ‒ ‒ ‒ ‒ ‒ ‒ ‒ ‒ ‒ ‒ ‒ ‒ ‒ ‒ ‒ ‒ ‒ ‒ ‒ ‒ ‒ ‒

‒ ‒ ‒ ‒ ‒ ‒ ‒ ‒ ‒ ‒ ‒ ‒ ‒ ‒ ‒ ‒ ‒ ‒ ‒ ‒ ‒ ‒ ‒ ‒ ‒ ‒

‒ ‒ ‒ ‒ ‒ ‒ ‒ ‒ ‒ ‒ ‒ ‒ ‒ ‒ ‒ ‒ ‒ ‒ ‒ ‒ ‒ ‒ ‒ ‒ ‒ ‒

‒ ‒ ‒ ‒ ‒ ‒ ‒ ‒ ‒ ‒ ‒ ‒ ‒ ‒ ‒ ‒ ‒ ‒ ‒ ‒ ‒ ‒ ‒ ‒ ‒ ‒

## Space to draw how you are feeling now:

# Part III:
# Approaching
# the loss experience
# through fiction

**Activity 15** Story time: Lilly has to say goodbye...

*Lilly feels hopeless, sad, and angry when she has to say goodbye to two of her siblings and to beloved Grandpa*

# Activity 15 Story time: Lilly has to say goodbye...

## Note to readers

Providing extended exercises for children who are transforming their losses, closures, or relationship endings is an important step to resolving their pain and reintegrating back into the world.

For children, providing activities that parallel their cognitive level through literature enables the healing process. Children enjoy reading about how other children or fictional characters have coped with their endings and closures. The experience is once removed from their own direct losses and is a way to handle better the overwhelming feelings they may encounter. It also gives a framework from which the child can identify and work through their feelings in play or experiential expression. With a new feelings vocabulary and a better ability to identify their own feelings through Part I and II exercises, the child can better express, identify, and transform their pain.

The short fiction story can be introduced at the beginning, middle, or end of the child's work or exercises. It can also be extended to include other stories about endings or loss. This work can additionally be extended into group work.

You may substitute the loss fictional story about Lilly for another if it is more meaningful to your child's circumstances. For example, the story in Activity 15 is about multiple losses that may occur in natural disasters but your child's experience may be divorce or a grandparent death. In this case, shape the fictional stories chosen to your child's circumstances.

The tools and templates section contains an extensive reading section for each age and reading level. A curriculum and guide is also provided at the end of the story section. Reading fiction is an important way to extend discussion and conversations for children. Your library may also help you with resources and books.

The story displaces the reality of endings through the use of fictional character. It also addresses the multiple losses that occur in the animal kingdom, one loss from a natural disaster, one from an accident, and one from old age.

There are natural disasters and accidents in the world today that cause multiple losses and some children do have to endure these types of traumas. Seek help from a professional psychologist or counselor to help you support the child who has experienced these special kinds of losses.

Children can relate to this story on several levels and it may serve as an ice-breaker for the child's own endings—human or animal—or as a way to introduce extended reading through bibliography. It also serves as a way to practice and learn new feeling words.

The story surrounds a family of skinks (from the lizard family), which are also endangered in the world today, but you can substitute this for an animal, insect, or toy that the child would better identify with, if preferred.

# Activity 15 Story time

## Lilly has to say goodbye...

Lilly has had to say goodbye to too many of her loved ones. She feels hopeless, sad, and angry when she has to say goodbye to them and to accept that she will not see them again in her lifetime.

What does she do with her strong feelings?

Where do they go? How long does it take?

How can she help resolve her own confused feelings?

I once had a friend, a small skink* ("skinks" come from the family of lizards). She lived at the bottom of my garden. My friend, Lilly, had a large family of sisters, brothers, aunts, uncles and grandparents living with her at the bottom of my garden.

Sadly, Lilly had endured the loss of the unthinkable, a brother, a sister, *and* her grand-father—he had been very old.

---

\* Please note that the skink featured in this fictional story is also an endangered species in the world today

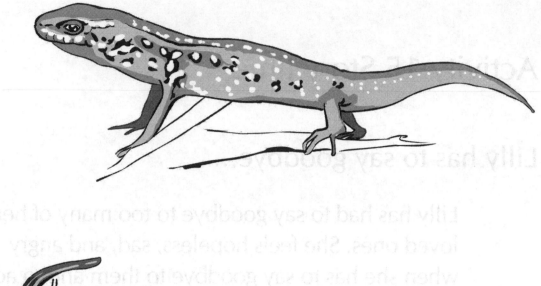

Her brother, Sunny had come to an untimely death when he was hunted by the neighbor's cat, Zin. Lilly's older sister, Rosie, had been washed away by a severe storm. She had not been found for over three months. Her parents called it a "natural disaster" but there was nothing natural about the feelings inside her.

Lilly felt *sad* when Grandpa died of old age but *angry* when both her brother and sister died. It didn't seem fair, they were both so young.

Lilly felt confused with strong feelings of disbelief, anger, frustration, and overwhelming sadness. She didn't know what she was feeling, or how to get it out. She felt like a volcano inside.

At night, she would let a tear flow down her face. She tried to be brave and not show her parents but at night, alone in her nest, she remembered the good times she had had with Grandpa, the everyday times with Sunny where they played and played in the tree tops high above human life.

She cried when she remembered her beloved sister, Rosie, especially at night when tucked into their nests they would exchange stories of their day.

Lilly felt like exploding, she felt so confused with strong feelings of anger, sadness, horror, fear. They were all jumbled up inside like she was inside a washing machine.

What could she do to help herself to feel better? How could she express all the jumbled up feelings she had inside?

Lilly talked to her wise grandmother who was also very sad about Grandpa, Rosie, and Sunny. Together they talked way into the night about the good times they had had with each of them. They cried over old photos, pored over old items that belonged to each of them—old clothes, photos, tickets, toys, and personal nick-nacks.

Lilly hugged Grandpa's old jacket close to her and smelled his scent. She longed to feel his strong arms wrap around her and lift her up high into the sky. She felt close to him this way and asked Grandma if she could keep his jacket close to her to snuggle into at night when she felt so lonely.

Lilly picked out several seashells that she and Rosie had picked out at the seashore when the family had gone to the seaside for a picnic. She could still smell the salty sea, and she rubbed the shell against her cheek to feel its roughness. She remembered how she and Rosie had combed the seashore together to find the most beautiful and shiny shells to add to their collection.

Lilly thought about Sunny. He had been so adorable as a little skink. She had felt so proud to have helped Mom feed and bathe him when he was tiny. She had held his hand when he learned to crawl along the treetops, and later run on all four legs.

Lilly had helped him to play baseball when he was a little bigger and they had played hide and seek for hours. She always let him win and he would shriek with delight at catching her out.

There were so many memories and so many confused feelings inside. Lilly drew and painted as much as she could remember. She celebrated the times they had together and put the pictures around her nest. She placed carefully the precious items she had collected: the seashells, the photos, the favorite toys that had belonged to Sunny.

Lilly placed them carefully on a shelf with photos of her sister, brother, and Grandpa. She placed small keepsakes in a special box and took them out often to look at them and remember...

Lilly wished her jumbled and confused feelings were over with after doing all of this, but they weren't.

There were many times over the next few weeks and months that she felt those strong, angry, sad, confused, and shocked feelings.

Sometimes she wanted to lash out and hurt someone to make them feel the pain she was feeling.

But instead Lilly went to her nest, she looked at the photos of her family, she talked with them as if they were still there, she opened the box of memories, and she felt the little toys in her hands that once belonged to her little brother.

Most of all she drew and painted. She painted all that was inside her at that moment. Lilly put it all down on paper.

Sometimes she wrote about her pain, sometimes she painted, sometimes she played her favorite DVDs and radio station. Another time she asked Dad to play baseball with her and she would hit the ball as hard as she could, running with all her might to the next base.

Sometimes these things helped, and sometimes they didn't... Sometimes all she could do was to hold up her hands and cry large, salty tears down her face. She would hold Grandpa's coat close to her and pretend he was giving her a big bear hug.

Lilly found it very hard to face Christmas, their birthdays, and her own birthday without them there to help plan and play at her party.

By the next spring, in the following year, Lilly found that her very strong and mixed-up feelings were starting to be less strong and instead she was feeling sadness. She cried often at the thought of Rosie, Sunny and Grandpa. It was a tragedy that she had lost three of her beloved family members but there were other things to celebrate...

Mom had had another baby. Lilly had a good friend at school and she had a few playtimes at her house. Lilly had started taking music lessons and loved playing the piano.

Little by little, Lilly left those difficult months behind her and the strong, confused feeling seemed to calm. Lilly became involved in many new activities and made new friends. She found she no longer needed to sit by her shelf in her nest to remember and feel the trinkets and toys she had placed to honor her relatives. It was a difficult time and although she would never forget, she could find contentment again in her life and with her new activities. This took time and patience and acceptance that it was alright to feel confused and scared and angry at times.

# Part IV:
# Creating groups

*Four-week curriculum*

# Introduction to the four-week curriculum

## Note to readers

This four-week curriculum guide is meant as a simple framework for educators, parents, and community groups to utilize to help children in their grief and loss. The group facilitator or leader needs to understand that they must provide a safe and private place for grief work to occur. Children cannot be pushed, forced, cajoled, or instructed on how to feel; they simply must be accepted for the space they are in and the feelings that accompany them. It is also important to remember that children, like adults, will transcend stages, regress, move forwards, backwards, skip stages, and move forward again. Respect for the dignity of the process needs to be exercised through acceptance of these stages.

Rules and structure for the group can be developed with the foundation principles of safety, confidentiality, permission not to share before they are ready, letting one child finish before they interrupt, listening while another is speaking, and the right to pass.

The group leader can facilitate opening and closing the group, help children set up and locate materials to carry through the activities, and facilitate the safety of the environment so that feelings can be shared.

Consider how many weeks the group will be running and the importance of screening the children prior to the start so that rapport can be built. Screening can be awkward and anxiety provoking, so it may be a good idea to have some manipulative materials available for children to work with as you lay the foundation for further grief work by building and establishing a trusting relationship. See the tools and templates section for a screening questionnaire, evaluation sheets, and handouts (see Appendix F).

It is also important to conduct a group with similar losses together, for example, a small group of children experiencing the death of a close family member, a small group of children experiencing divorce. It is better not to mix together children who are dealing with different types of losses.

It is better to start a child in a loss group three months after the loss, because earlier than this, the child may be too shocked and numb to really be able to get anything out of the activities. In this case, individual support would be better until another, later group is available.

Consider whether you will have a co-facilitator, the time, and location of the group (consider privacy and confidentiality). Also consider recruiting staff to help children get to the group quickly if the group is being conducted in school time.

## Structure of the group

The group will have the following components:

- a theme with the objectives of the group facilitated through expressive activities

- an opening ritual that is consistent each time the group opens. After the greeting, group rules and norms can be addressed. Introductions to the exercises and activities can be approached at this point with directions about how and where to access material needed

- one of two exercises to be worked through each week

- handouts

- a closing ritual that is consistent each time the group closes. It is important to give plenty of time at the end of the group to help younger children make the transition into their next class or activity. By asking children ten minutes ahead of the end of the group how they are coping will provide them with time and opportunity to share, if they wish, and also will help to bring them back into the reality of their schedules. This can be accompanied by going over a handout, asking them what was helpful in this week's group, and asking them to share one or two elements or tools they learned in the group setting that they can take away into the following weeks.

## Weekly group themes

Each week there will be similar themes, for example:

- opening: introduction and groundbreaking exercises
- sharing memories activity
- feeling activities
- coping tools
- goodbyes and memorials.

# Special topics in groups

(This may need to be considered by a facilitator before starting the group and in the pre-screening and planning stage.)

## *Anger and sadness*

These two emotions are necessary for the grieving process. Children may display either and the facilitator's acceptance of these emotions must be appropriate. Helping children to express their pain is part of the facilitator's role. Children can be comforted and allowed to express their concerns and emotions. Other children in the group can also be encouraged to express empathy towards other group members.

If you feel at any time that the depth of emotion, or lack of emotion is inappropriate, consultation with a counselor, therapist, psychologist, psychiatrist, or social worker may be required. Remember that children regress, skip, and move through the grief process at their own pace and not yours. Participation in a group may be the catalyst for further feeling work.

## Traumatic loss

Traumatic losses in children may present in different ways than in adults. Identifying eight of the symptoms for post traumatic stress disorder involves giving a verbal description of feelings and experiences. Young children who do not have the developmental skills to verbalize these symptoms may instead present with symptomology of general fears, separation anxiety, or avoidance. Young children may also experience sleep problems or obsessive occupation with words or symbols related to the disorder. Play may include repetitive play of the trauma in which themes of the trauma are repeated. Children may also regress in their development.

Children may become hypervigilant to warning signs of any future traumas. School-age children may re-enact the trauma through play, drawing, or verbalization. Some children may also compulsively repeat some aspect of the trauma but it will not help to reduce their anxiety.

Though its symptoms can occur soon after the event, the disorder often surfaces several months or even years later.

Parents and caregivers should be alert to the following changes in a *child's behavior*:

- refusal to return to school and "clinging" behavior, including shadowing the mother or father around the house

- persistent fears related to the catastrophe (such as fears about being permanently separated from parents)

- sleep disturbances such as nightmares, screaming during sleep and bedwetting, persisting more than several days after the event

- loss of concentration and irritability

- startled easily, jumpy

- behavior problems, for example, misbehaving in school or at home in ways that are not typical for the child

- physical complaints (stomach aches, headaches, dizziness) for which a physical cause cannot be found

- withdrawal from family and friends, sadness, listlessness, decreased activity, and preoccupation with the events of the disaster.

Seek professional advice or treatment for children affected by a disaster, especially those who have witnessed destruction, injury, or death. Depression and anxiety (viewed as separation anxiety, panic disorder, generalized anxiety disorder, or withdrawal) often accompany post traumatic stress disorder.

Children who are having serious problems with *grief* and *loss* may show one or more of these signs:

- an extended period of depression in which the child loses interest in daily activities and events

- inability to sleep, loss of appetite, prolonged fear of being alone

- acting much younger for an extended period

- excessively imitating the dead person

- repeated statements of wanting to join the dead person

- withdrawal from friends, or

- sharp drop in school performance or refusal to attend school.

If these signs persist, professional help may be needed.

## Symptoms and behaviors associated with depression in children

- crying, feeling sad, helpless, or hopeless

- feeling discouraged or worthless

- loss of interest or pleasure in others or most activities

- fatigue and loss of energy nearly every day

- bad temper, irritable, easily annoyed

- fearful, tense, anxious

- repeated rejection by other children

- drop in school performance

- inability to sit still, fidgeting or pacing

- repeated emotional outbursts, shouting, or complaining

- not talking to other children

- repeated physical complaints without medical cause (headaches, stomach aches, aching arms or legs)

- significant increase or decrease in appetite (not due to appropriate dieting)

- change in sleep habits.

## Serious and critical symptoms

- suicidal thoughts, feelings, or self-harming behavior

- abuse or prolonged use of alcohol or other drugs

- symptoms of depression combined with strange or unusual behavior.

# Four-week curriculum structure

## Week 1 Laying the foundation for feeling work

A few weeks prior to the group, you may wish to invite children to bring a memory item that belonged to the person or pet that is deceased.

*Openings* Introductions, ice-breakers, group guidelines, development of group rules, sharing, making the native sharing stick

*Native Sharing Stick Activity* (to be used at the beginning of each group session)

*Activity 1* Creating a safe place to be

*Activity 2* Feeling puzzle

*Activity 3* Match the feeling game

*Activity 4* Faces collage

*Activity 5* Feeling faces

*Transitions to closure* Circle fictional story time

*Closings* It is important to give plenty of time to bring closure to the group and to check in with children that have been quiet or emotional.

# Week 2 Developing emotional literacy

*Openings*

*Native sharing stick activity*

*Activity* 6 Feeling words

*Activity* 7 Finish the sentence...

*Activity* 8 What color are my feelings?

*Activity* 9 Feelings rainbow

*Transitions to closure* Circle fictional story time

*Closings* Check in with children and ask them to help you clean up the supplies. Remind children that there are two more meetings.

# Week 3 Learning about relationship goodbyes, closures, and endings

*Openings*

*Native sharing stick activity*

*Activity 10* Saying goodbye is hard to do...

*Activity 11* Talking about losses of pets or toys (optional depending on group needs)

*Activity 12* Good memories

*Activity 13* Memory boxes

*Activity 14* New perspectives (may also be used as an evaluation for group work; an evaluation form can be found in Appendix F)

*Transition to closure* Circle fictional story time

*Closings* Check in with children, remind them to bring their memory boxes next week and that next week's group is the last group meeting.

# Week 4 Learning to bring closure through behavior

*Openings*

*Native sharing stick activity*

*Activity 14* New Perspectives (may serve as an evaluation of group).
Ask the children to complete this activity if they did not complete it in the previous week.

*Activity 15* Circle fictional story about "Lilly".
Discussion about losses and feelings around the losses, sharing of memory boxes, and why you chose the items to put in your memory box. Review of feelings discussed, recognition of different spectrums of feelings, and new vocabulary of words.

*Closings* Goodbyes. Handouts may be given to parents or caregivers regarding depression, traumatic loss, and grief. Identification of resources for support and what help is available in the tools and templates section. Handouts can be found in Appendix E.

# Description of weekly group activities

*Openings* (Group activity performed at the beginning of each week)

## *Native sharing stick activity*

> This activity is performed in a group and the facilitator can explain the objective of the activity as the group is creating the sharing stick.

## *Materials*

> Find a cardboard tube similar to the type that wrapping paper is rolled around, or a paper towel tube (although this may be too short). The longer the tube the better so that children can easily grasp and pass on the "stick" to another child in the circle. In the middle of the circle, have craft materials already cut and prepared and ready to be glued to the cardboard tube. Craft materials to be glued can include beads, fur, and feathers. For younger children, choose your materials to match developmental abilities (hand—eye coordination, perception, safety of materials used). Have plenty of white glue available for adhering the materials to the tube.

## Goals

- To utilize a symbol that will serve as an ice-breaker and help children feel safe in their environment.

- To develop verbal, listening, and turn-taking skills.

- To encourage the development and identification of feelings.

## Description

Gather children in a circle. This can be performed on the floor or at a table. Have craft materials in the middle of the circle or table. Explain to the children that in native cultures, a talking stick was brought to important meetings to help members speak with courage and truth. In this group, the stick will be used at the beginning of the meetings each week and will be passed from one child to another. When the stick is passed to one of the children, they will be gently directed to glue some of the materials to it and share with others what brought them to the group. When the child has finished sharing, they can pass the stick on to the next child in the circle.

In this way, the decoration of the stick will be completed after the circle is finished and each week thereafter, the stick will be completed and passed around the circle to share feelings and new developments in the grief process.

Remember that each child has the right to pass on sharing their feelings and this activity is voluntary. Sharing can be started by the facilitator, as the facilitator, will need to role model the ways in which words and feelings may be shared.

The facilitator can also explain the symbolism of the craft materials included: feathers represent truth in words, fur represents the animals or the earth, and the beads represent people of the earth.

## Transitions

After you have completed this opening activity, you may transition to the next exercises. Remember that transitions can cause some children difficulty, so allow them to find a quiet or cozy place to sit and observe until they are ready to participate. You can also encourage participants to bring their favorite toy with them to cuddle or hold during emotional times.

# Week 1 activities

## ACTIVITY 1 CREATING A SAFE PLACE TO BE (EXPRESSIVE ACTIVITY)

*Goals*

- To create a place of environmental and emotional safety in which to explore feeling work.

- To create a sense of group belonging.

*Materials*

Photocopies of exercises, paints, crayons, colored pencils, colored markers. Have plenty of paper and coloring materials available so that children can explore with a variety of mediums and start over again if they wish.

*Description*

Utilizing the exercise in Activity 1, ask the children to create a picture of where they feel safe. (Children may wish to draw on the floor, and should be encouraged to create where and how they feel most comfortable.)

ACTIVITY 2 FEELING PUZZLE
ACTIVITY 3 MATCH THE FEELING GAME
ACTIVITY 4 FACES COLLAGE

## Goals

- Lay the foundation for children to recognize and identify feelings.

- Develop feeling words vocabulary.

- Develop the recognition of correct feelings on faces.

- Develop empathy skills.

## Materials

Photocopies of Activity 2 and 3, crayons, pencils, paints, brushes, markers, felt tips, scissors, old magazines, glue.

## Description

Read together the feeling sentences. Very young children with emerging reading skills can be read to in a circle and then invited to draw a simple line to match the feeling words that are jumbled. Pay attention to children that have difficulty recognizing the "jealous" face and those who switch the "angry" face for a "sad" face. For young children the distinctions between the two are often difficult.

This activity can lead to a discussion on how it is often difficult to recognize a feeling when you are viewing the expression on a face in a picture in a magazine, on television, or on a real person. You can invite the children to mimic these emotions on their faces in a dramatic way.

In Activity 4, children are invited to cut out faces (not bodies) that are expressing some of the emotions that have recently been discussed. Some children will incorrectly identify an emotion expressed on a face as they are still learning to recognize that feeling in others. This can lead to further discussion about facial expressions.

## ACTIVITY 5 FEELING FACES (EXPRESSIVE ACTIVITY)

### Goals

- Extend Activity 3 to identify feeling words to match illustrated faces.

- Extend and develop the feelings vocabulary.

- Socialize children to alternative words that mean the same as "happy."

### Cultural tip

Children will know and be comfortable with different types of feeling names dependent on their culture. For example, children from European cultures may be comfortable with and have an understanding of words such as "glad" whereas a child from a North American culture may be more at ease with "awesome." You can extend this activity by discussing the different cultural words used in society today and have the children explore what words are most utilized in their own culture.

### Materials

Crayons, pencils, markers, felt tips, paints.

## Description

This exercise builds and develops Activity 3 in which the child was invited to draw a line to match up the feeling word to correctly illustrate facial expression. In this activity, the *feeling word*, not the illustrated face, is matched to the child's own drawing of the face. The child will need to identify the feeling word and appropriately create a drawing of the words "joyful," "ecstatic," "glad," "awesome." These alternative words to "happy" help to develop the feelings vocabulary.

# Week 2 activities

## ACTIVITY 6 FEELING WORDS (WRITTEN EXERCISES)

*Goals*

- Builds on the feeling words of "happy," "sad," "angry," and "frightened."

- Builds emotional literacy.

- Helps children to identify and comprehend similar feeling words.

- Develops ability to use feeling words correctly in context.

*Materials*

Photocopies of Activity 6 and feelings vocabulary list, crayons, pencils, markers, felt tips.

*Description*

Introduce the feelings vocabulary list and read out alternative words under each of the four columns. Ask the children to think of any other words that are not listed that also mean "happy," "sad," "angry," "scared." Have them write the words under the last words listed in each column (here the child may offer culturally appropriate feeling words not listed in the vocabulary list). Ask each child also to list in the blank provided their chosen alternative feeling word. For example, under the heading "sad words," a list of three alternative sad words are offered. Have the child identify one more "sad" word from the feeling vocabulary list, or one of their own.

## Note to readers

Some children will use the word "depressed" for "sad." In a clinical sense, "depressed" does not mean the literal word for "sad" but it is common to hear such words used when describing sad feelings.

## ACTIVITY 7 FINISH THE SENTENCE (WRITTEN EXERCISE)

### Goals

- Help children to recognize and comprehend appropriate feeling words in context.

- Help children to identify, recognize, and label darker emotions.

### Materials

Photocopies of Activity 7, crayons, colored pencils, pencils, markers, felt tips.

### Description

Invite the children to read over the sentences provided in Activity 7. Ask them to think of an appropriate feeling word to write in the blank provided.

## ACTIVITY 8 WHAT COLOR ARE MY FEELINGS?
## ACTIVITY 9 FEELINGS RAINBOW

### Goals

- Helps children to identify the color they use to express emotions in expressive art work.

- Individualizes the expressive work.

### Materials

Paints, brushes, crayons, colored pencils, pencils, markers, felt tips.

### Description

Invite the children to read the sentences together in the group and then pick a color that matches their own individual feeling. Encourage them to use whatever color they wish and not to copy their neighbor. For example, red does not have to represent anger. Children can individualize whatever color they choose and the colors picked may not match the way colors are stereotypically represented in society. Do not lead the child to pick a color but encourage them to choose whatever color *feels* similar to the written feeling.

Similarly with constructing the rainbow, invite the children to transfer the colors they originally chose to color the boxes into the colors of the feeling rainbow. For example, if the color pink was chosen to identify the child's "hurt" color, this color can now be used to create the feeling rainbow for the band that is identified as the "hurt" band. The child therefore colors one band a pink color. Finish the rainbow in a similar way with a different color representing the different emotions of anger, hurt, sad, happy, jealous, frustrated, and scared.

# Week 3 activities

## ACTIVITY 10 SAYING GOODBYE IS HARD TO DO

### Goals

- Help children to recognize everyday closures.

- Help children to express everyday closures.

### Materials

Photocopies of Activity 10, crayons, paints, brushes, markers, pencils, felt tips, colored pencils.

### Description

Activity 10 develops the child's ability to recognize their own closures and to express these goodbyes through art. Discussion of goodbyes can be extended to each child as they share their drawings and paintings with the group. This activity can bring up deeper emotions and perhaps difficult behaviors, so it is important to check in with each child prior to the group ending and provide some grounding exercises at the end. Ask the children to help you clean up and put away the materials. Ask them to bring a special item that belongs to the person and reminds them of the loss.

## ACTIVITY 11 TALKING ABOUT LOSSES OF PETS OR TOYS

### Goals

- To provide a special recognition of pet or toy losses and the memories that children hold dear about them.

- To provide children with an expressive area to visually create the loss.

Activity 11 can be extended, if needed, to include Activity 12 to 14 in which memories are gathered and a memory box created.

### Materials

Photocopies of Activity 11, pencils, pencil crayons, colored markers, felt tips, paints, brushes, glue (if using photos).

### Description

If the loss represents a pet or toy, the children can write in the space provided and draw or paint a drawing of the loss. Alternatively, children can bring in a photo of the pet or toy and glue it into the activity box.

## ACTIVITY 12 GOOD MEMORIES

### Goals

To gather items that remind the child of the loss or belonged to the person who is being remembered, for example, photos, memorabilia, personal belongings owned by the person that are meaningful to the child.

### Materials

Items collected are the child's choice, but could include:

- photos

- pictures/drawings

- small items—keys, balls, tickets to community or recreational activities attended, accessories worn

- clothing

- personal nick-nacks

- part of collections or hobbies pursued

- printed works

- dried flowers or leaves.

There are no limits to the items brought but if the child is making a memory box, space may need to be considered.

## Description

To gather symbols that remind children of the loss and times shared together. There are no limits to what can be brought to the group to make memory boxes but the facilitator will need to keep the items secure as children construct their boxes. Some children will wish to use the creative drawings and writings they have developed through these exercises, while other children may wish to create new drawings or writings to place in their boxes.

## ACTIVITY 13 MEMORY BOXES

### Goals

- To develop a concrete symbol of the loss.

- To create a place of honor and love for the loss.

- To develop concrete ways to transcend the reality of the loss.

### Materials

A container, a shelf, a box, a scrapbook that can be used to put symbolic memorabilia or items inside. Some craft stores sell memory boxes with a glass front on them so that the items can be displayed but this is not necessary. A shoebox, small, lidded container, and space on a bookshelf can all be created to honor these special items. Other materials include scissors, paint, white glue, paint brushes, colored markers, felt tips, pencils.

When the child has gathered all the memorabilia, photos, and nick-nacks they wish to display, ask them to first decorate the outside of the container if they wish and to line the inside with scrap materials or paint inside.

When the memory container is dry (this activity may extend to the next session), ask the children to gently place the items inside. If the child is concerned about them slipping around inside the container, you can glue them down.

When the children have completed the memory boxes, they can sit in a circle and either individually, or as a group, say the mantra, "I will always remember you, please take care and know you will always be in my memories." Children can cuddle the soft toys they have brought with them if they become upset. Let the children know that this memory box is their own to put wherever they wish, perhaps in a bedroom, or on a shelf. The point is that this box and the items inside can be opened, looked at, touched and handled whenever they wish. These symbolic memories are theirs to access and treasure forever.

# Week 4 activities

## ACTIVITY 14 NEW PERSPECTIVES (WRITTEN AND EXPRESSIVE ACTIVITY)

### Goals

- To bring closure, or, to use the group work as a foundation for other extended work.

- To build a foundation for generating new perspectives on and around the loss.

- To reintegrate feelings of loss to feelings of acceptance or new beginnings.

- To utilize this activity as a simple evaluation or progress activity to observe how the child has developed and created new ways to view the loss.

### Materials

Photocopies of Activity 14, pencils, crayons, colored pencils, markers, felt tips, paints, and brushes.

## Description

Ask the children to think of new or different *feeling* words they have learned since the group's inception. This activity also asks the child to express in words and through drawings, how they feel about the loss *now*. This will give the facilitator a chance to observe the underlying emotions about the grief process and if the child will need extended activities. For example, if the child is expressing resolution, the group may be all that is needed but if the child is expressing anger or sadness, more support—individual or group support—may be required.

# ACTIVITY 15 APPROACHING THE LOSS EXPERIENCE THROUGH FICTION

## Goals

- To help children relate to the loss through fictional characters which may be less threatening to them.

- To use fiction as a catalyst in which children can also express their feelings around the loss.

- To socialize children to the reality of life and death in society.

- To extend the use of fiction in the lives of children experiencing overwhelming feelings.

## Materials

Photocopies of Activity 15, fictional story about multiple losses in the animal kingdom.

## Description

The children can sit in a circle to read this short story. This is a story of multiple losses in the animal kingdom. The story illustrates, through fiction, how the character overcomes feelings of grief. The story illustrates that there is no "quick fix" for grief and that it is normal to experience deep, conflicting emotions at such a time. The story also develops over time so that the reader develops an understanding of the resolution of emotion. The story also offers hope for the reader in how the future unfolds for the character.

# Tools and templates

**Appendix A**  Cover page to be used if the exercises are to be made into a personalized book

**Appendix B**  Feelings vocabulary list

**Appendix C**  UK, EU, US and Canadian resources; International web resources

**Appendix D**  Recommended reading

**Appendix E**  Handout 1 Children's common reactions to traumatic stress; Handout 2 Signs of serious problems with grief and loss; Handout 3 Symptoms and behaviors associated with depression in children; Handout 4 How teachers can help children deal with grief and loss

**Appendix F**  Group screening questionnaire; Group evaluation activity; About the author

# Appendix A

To be used if exercises are made into a book for the child.

This book belongs to

This is a picture or photo of me

# Appendix B

## Feelings vocabulary list

| Feelings vocabulary | | | |
|---|---|---|---|
| **Happy** | **Sad** | **Angry** | **Scared** |
| Excited | Hopeless | Furious | Terrified |
| Overjoyed | Sorrowful | Seething | Petrified |
| Elated | Depressed | Enraged | Alarmed |
| Great | Lonely | Fuming | Panicked |
| Ecstatic | Discouraged | Bitter | Fearful |
| Cheerful | Down | Annoyed | Afraid |
| Joyful | Miserable | Frustrated | Anxious |
| Delighted | Low | Irritated | Nervous |

# Appendix C

## UK and EU resources

**CLIC Sargent (Caring for Children with Cancer)**
Hammersmith Office
Griffin House
161 Hammersmith Road
London W6 8SG
Tel: 020 8752 2800
Fax: 020 8752 2806
Website: www.clicsargent.org.uk

**The Child Bereavement Charity**
Aston House
West Wycombe
High Wycombe
Bucks HP14 3AG
Tel: 01494 446648
Email: enquiries@childbereavement.org.uk
Website: www.childbereavement.org.uk

**Childline**
Free phone helpline for children (24 hours a day):
0800 1111
Tel: 020 7239 1000
Website: www.childline.org.uk

**European Association for Palliative Care**
EAPC Head Office
National Cancer Institute Milano
Via Venezia 1
20133 Milano
Italy
Tel: +39 02 2390 3390
Fax: +39 02 2390 3393
Website: www.eapcnet.org

**Grief Encounter Project**
P.O. Box 49701
London, N20 8XJ
Tel: 020 8446 7452
Email: contact@griefencounter.com
Website: www.griefencounter.com

**National Association of Widows**
3rd Floor
48 Queens Road
Coventry CV1 3EH
Tel: 0845 838 2261
Email: info@nawidows.org.uk
Website: www.nawidows.org.uk

**The National Council for Palliative Care**
The Fitzpatrick Building
188–194 York Way
London N7 9AS
Tel: 020 7697 1520
Fax: 020 7697 1530
Email: enquiries@ncpc.org.uk
Website: www.ncpc.org.uk

**SupportLine**
P.O. Box 1596
Ilford
Essex IG1 3FW
Tel: 020 8554 9006
Helpline: 020 8554 9004
Email: info@supportline.org.uk
Website: www.supportline.org.uk

**Youth Involvement Project**
Cruse Bereavement Care
PO Box 800
Richmond
Surrey TW9 1RG
Tel: 020 8939 9530
Fax: 020 8940 1671
Email: info@rd4u.org.uk
Website: www.rd4u.org.uk
Free phone helpline: 0808 808 1677

# US resources

**AARP**
601 E Street NW
Washington
DC 20049
US
Website: www.aarp.org/families/grief_loss

**Academy of Cognitive Therapy**
One Belmont Avenue, Suite 700
Bala Cynwyd
PA 19004-1610
Tel: (610) 664 1273
Fax: (610) 664 5137
Email: info@academyofct.org
Website: www.academyofct.org

**American Academy of Child and Adolescent Psychiatry**
3615 Wisconsin Avenue NW
Washington
DC 20016-3007
Tel: (202) 966 7300
Website: www.aacap.org

**American Academy of Hospice and Palliative Medicine**
4700 W Lake Avenue
Glenview
IL 60025-1485
Tel: (847) 375 4712
Fax: (877) 734 8671
Email: info@aahpm.org
Website: www.aahpm.org

**American Association for Marriage and Family Therapy**
112 South Alfred Street
Alexandria
VA 22314-3061
Tel: (703) 838 9808
Fax: (703) 838 9805
Website: www.aamft.org

**American Counseling Association**
5999 Stevenson Avenue
Alexandria
VA 22304
Tel: (800) 347 6647
Fax: (800) 473 2329
TDD: 703.823 6862
Website: www.counseling.org

**American Foundation for Suicide Prevention**
120 Wall Street, 22nd Floor
New York
NY 10005
Tel: (212) 363 3500
Fax: (212) 363 6237
Toll free: 1 888 333 AFSP
Email: inquiry@afsp.org
Website: www.afsp.org

**American Psychiatric Association**
1000 Wilson Boulevard, Suite 1825
Arlington
VA 22209-3901
Tel: (703) 907 7300
Email: apa@psych.org
Website: www.psych.org

**American Psychological Association**
750 First St, NE, Suite 700
Washington
DC 20002-4242
Tel: (202) 336 5500
Website: www.apa.org

**American School Counselor Association**
1101 King Street, Suite 625
Alexandria
VA 22314
Tel: (703) 683 ASCA
Fax: (703) 683 1619
Toll free: (800) 306 4722
Website: www.schoolcounselor.org

**American Society of Clinical Oncology**
1900 Duke Street, Suite 200
Alexandria
VA 22314
Tel: (703) 299 0150
Fax: (703) 299 1044
Email: asco@asco.org
Website: www.asco.org

**Anxiety Disorders Association of America**
8730 Georgia Avenue, Suite 600
Silver Spring
MD 20910
Tel: (240) 485 1001
Fax: (240) 485 1035
Website: www.adaa.org

**Association for Play Therapy**
2060 N. Winery Avenue, #102
Fresno
CA 93703
Tel: (559) 252 2278
Fax: (559) 252 2297
Email: info@a4pt.org
Website: www.a4pt.org

**Mental Health America**
2000 N Beauregard Street, 6th Floor
Alexandria
VA 22311
Tel: (703) 684 7722
Fax: (703) 684 5968
Toll free: (800) 969 6642
TTY line (800) 433 5959
Website: www.nmha.org

**NACBT**
P.O. Box 2195
Weirton
WV 26062
Tel: (800) 853 1135
Fax: (304) 723 3982
Email: nacbt@nacbt.org
Website: www.nacbt.org

**National Association for Drama Therapy**
15 Post Side Lane
Pittsford
NY 14534
Tel: (585) 381 5618
Fax: (585) 383 1474
Website: www.nadt.org

**National Association for Poetry Therapy**
Lauren Keller
CETHA
777 E Atlantic Avenue, #243
Delray Beach
FL 33483
Tel: (561) 498 8334
Toll free: 1 866 844 NAPT
Fax: (561) 495 1877
Website: www.poetrytherapy.org

**National Association of School Psychologists**
4340 East West Highway, Suite 402
Bethesda
MD 20814
Tel: (301) 657 0270
Website: www.nasponline.org

**National Cancer Institute**
Cancer Information Service
Tel: (800) 422 6237
Website: www.cancer.gov

**National Center for Complimentary and Alternative Medicine**
National Institutes of Health
9000 Rockville Pike
Bethesda
MD 20892
Tel: (301) 519 3153
Email: info@nccam.nih.gov
Website: www.nccam.nih.gov

**National Center for Posttraumatic Stress Disorder**
Tel: (802) 296 6300 (Information line)
Email: ncptsd@va.gov
Website: www.ncptsd.va.gov

**National POMC**
100 East Eighth Street, Suite 202
Cincinnati
OH 45202
Email: natlpomc@aol.com
Tel: (513) 721 5683
Fax: (513) 345 4489
Toll free: (888) 818 POMC
Website: www.pomc.com

**SAVE–Suicide Awareness Voices of Education**
8120 Penn Avenue S
Suite 470
Bloomington
MN 55431
Tel: (952) 946 7998
Website: www.save.org

**Sidran Institute**
200 East Joppa Road, Suite 207
Baltimore
MD 21286-3107
Tel: (410) 825 8888
Website: www.sidran.org

# Canadian resources

**Canadian Art Therapy Association**
26 Earl Grey Rd
Toronto
ON M4J 3L2
Website: www.catainfo.ca

**Canadian Association for Child and Play Therapy**
329 March Road
Suite 232, Box 11
Ottawa
ON K2K 2E1
Toll free: (800) 361 3951
Fax: (613) 599 7027
Email: membership@cacpt.com
Website: www.cacpt.com

**The Canadian Association for Music Therapy**
Wilfred Laurier University
Waterloo
ON N2L 3C5
Tel: (519) 884 1970 ext. 6828
Toll free: 1 800 996 2268
Fax: (519) 886 9351
Email: camt@musictherapy.ca
Website: www.musictherapy.ca

**Canadian Association of School Psychologists**
CASP Executive Director
10660 Trepassey Drive
Richmond, British Columbia V7E 4K7
Email: casp.exec@gmail.com
Website: www.cpa.ca/CASP

**The Canadian Centre for Bereavement Education and Grief Counselling**
49 Gloucester Street
Toronto
ON M4Y 1L8
Tel: (416) 926 0905

**Canadian Counselling Association**
16 Concourse Gate, Suite 600
Ottawa
ON K2E 7S8
Toll free: 1 877 765 5565
Fax: (613) 237 9786
Email: info@ccacc.ca
Website: www.ccacc.ca

**Canadian Horticultural Therapy Association**
100 Westmount Road
Guelph
ON N1H 5H8
Email: admin@chta.ca
Website: www.chta.ca

**Canadian Hospice Palliative Care Association**
Annex B
Saint-Vincent Hospital
60 Cambridge Street North
Ottawa
ON K1R 7A
Tel: (613) 241 3663
Fax: (613) 241 3986
Hospice Palliative Care Info Line:
1 877 203 4636
Email: info@chpca.net
Website: www.chcpa.net

**Canadian Mental Health Association, Ontario**
180 Dundas Street West, Suite 2301
Toronto
ON M5G 1Z8
Tel: (416) 977 5580
Fax: (416) 977 2813
Toll free in Ontario: 1 800 875 6213
Email: info@ontario.cmha.ca
Website: www.ontario.cmha.ca

**Canadian Professional Counsellors Association**
#203, 3306 32nd Avenue
Vernon
BC V1T 2M6
Tel: 1 888 945 2722
Email: jgwright@telus.net or krystyh@telus.net
Website: www.cpca-rpc.ca

**The Canadian Psychiatric Association**
141 Laurier Avenue West, Suite 701
Ottawa
ON K1P 5J3
Tel: 613 234 2815
Fax: 613 234 9857
Email: cpa@cpa-apc.org
Website: www.cpa-apc.org

**Canadian Psychological Association**
141 Laurier Avenue West, Suite 702
Ottawa
ON K1P 5J3
Tel: (613) 237 2144
Fax: (613) 237 1674
Toll free: 1 888 472 0657
Email: cpa@cpa.ca
Website: www.cpa.ca

**Canadian Red Cross**
National Office
170 Metcalfe Street, Suite 300
Ottawa, Ontario
K2P 2P2
Tel: (613) 740 1900
Fax: (613) 740 1911
Email: feedback@redcross.ca
Website: www.redcross.ca

**Canadian Social Workers Association**
383 Parkdale Avenue, Suite 402
Ottawa
ON K1Y 4R4
Tel: (613) 729 6668
Fax: (613) 729 9608
Website: www.casw-acts.ca

**Canadian Society of Palliative Care Physicians**
c/o Grey Nuns Hospital
217 Health Service Centre
1090 Youville Drive West
Edmonton, AB
Tel: (780) 735 7727

Fax: (780) 735 7302
Email: Kathy.Robertstad@capitalhealth.ca
Website: www.cspcp.ca

**Centre for Suicide Prevention**
1202 Centre Street SE, Suite 320
Calgary
AB T2G 5A5
Tel: (403) 245 3900
Fax: (403) 245 0299
Email: esp@suicideinfo.ca
Website: www.suicideinfo.ca

**Mothers Against Drunk Driving**
2010 Winston Park Drive
Suite 500
Oakville
ON, 6H 5R7
Website: www.madd.ca

**Nova Scotia Hospice Palliative Care Association**
c/o Colchester Regional Hospital
207 Willow Street
Truro
NS B2N 5A1
Tel: 1 902 893 7171
Fax: 1 902 893 7172
Email: nshpca@eastlink.ca
Website: www.nshpca.ca

# International web resources

**ADEC Headquarters**
60 Revere Drive, Suite 500
Northbrook
IL 60062
US
Tel: (847) 509 0403
Fax: (847) 480 9282
Website: www.adec.org

**IASP**
Central Administrative Office
Le Barade
F-32330 Gondrin
France
Tel: +33 562 29 19 47
Fax: +33 562 29 19 47
Email: iasp1960@aol.com
Website: www.med.uio.no/iasp

## Memorial sites

**A Place to Remember**
www.aplacetoremember.com/
griefwww.html

**The Compassionate Friends of Canada**
www.tcfcanada.net

## Grief information and resources

**Beyond Indigo**
www.beyondindigo.com

**KA**
www.kidsaid.com

**KARA**
457 Kingsley Avenue
Palo Alto
CA 94301
US
Tel: (650) 321 5272
Website: www.kara-grief.org

**Centering Corporation**
7230 Maple Street
Omaha, Nebraska 68134
US
Toll free: 866 218 0101
Website: www.centeringcorp.com

**Compassion Books**
7036 State Highway 80 South
Burnsville
NC 28714
US
Toll free: 1 800 970 4220
Website: www.compassionbooks.com

**The Dougy Center**
PO Box 86852
Portland
OR 97286
US
Toll free: 866 775 5683
Website: www.dougy.org

**GriefNet**
PO Box 3272
Ann Arbor
MI 48106-3272
US
Website: www.griefnet.org

**Jessica Kingsley Publishers**
116 Pentonville Road
London N1 9JB
UK
Tel: 020 7833 2307
Fax: 020 7837 2917
Email: post@jkp.com
Website: www.jkp.com

**MISS Foundation**
PO Box 5333
Peoria
AZ 85385
US
Tel: (623) 979 1000
Fax: (623) 979 1001
Toll free: 1 888 455 MISS (in US)
Email: info@missfoundation.org
Website: www.missfoundation.org

**Canadian Foundation for the Study of Infant Deaths**
60 James Street, Suite 403
St. Catharines
ON L2R 7E7
Canada
Tel: (905) 688 8884
Fax: (905) 688 3300
Toll Free: 1 800 363 7437
Email: sidsinfo@sidscanada.org
Website: www.sidscanada.org

**Solace House**
8012 State Line Road, Suite 202
Shawnee Mission
KS 66208
US
Tel: (913) 341 0318
Fax: (913) 341 0319
Email: shmail@solacehouse.org
Website: www.solacehouse.org

# Palliative care

**Children's Hospice International**
1101 King Street, Suite 360
Alexandria
VA 22314
US
Tel: (703) 684 0330
Website: www.chionline.org

**Canadian Network for Palliative Care for Children**
Website: www.cnpcc.ca

**International Association for Hospice and Palliative Care**
5535 Memorial Drive,
Suite F-PMB 509
Houston
TX 77007
US
Tel: (936) 321 9846
Fax: (713) 880 2948
Toll free: (866) 374 2472
Website: www.hospicecare.com

**Perinatal Bereavement Services Ontario**
6060 Highway 7, Suite 205
Markham
ON L3P 3A9
Canada
Tel: (905) 472 1807
Fax: (905) 472 4054
Toll free: 1 888 301 PBSO (7276)
Email: pbsocares@pbso.ca
Website: www.pbso.ca

**Growth House**
Website: www.growthhouse.org

# Traumatic loss

**Civitas**
2210 W North Avenue
Chicago
IL 60647
US
Tel: (312) 226 6700
Website: www.civitas.org

**Gift from Within**
16 Cobb Hill Road
Camden
ME 04843
US
Tel: (207) 236 8858
Fax: (207) 236 2818
Email: JoyceB3955@aol.com
Website: www.giftfromwithin.org

## Practitioners

Website: www.thecbtcoach.com
Website: http://grieftopeace.com

## Audio programs

**Hayhouse Radio**
Website: www.hayhouseradio.com

**Psychjourney Audio Book Club**
Website: http://psychjourney_blogs.typepad.com

**The Grief Blog**
Website: http://thegriefblog.com

## Children's mental health

**KidsHealth**
Website: www.kidshealth.org/kid/feeling

**KidsPeace**
Website: www.kidspeace.org/resources.htm

**MentalHelp**
Website: www.mentalhelp.net

**School Psychology Resources Online**
Website: www.schoolpsychology.net

# Appendix D

## Recommended reading

### Children, 4–8 years

Adams, J. (2007) *The Dragonfly Door*. Maple Plain, MN: Feather Rock Books.

Attig, T. (1996) *How We Grieve: Relearning the World*. New York, NY: Oxford University Press.

Brown, L. and Brown, M. (1996) *When Dinosaurs Die: A Guide to Understanding Death*. New York, NY: Little, Brown.

Carney, K. (2001) *Barklay and Eve: Explaining Cancer to Children*. Weathersfield, CT: Dragonfly Publishing.

Cohn, J. and G. (1987) *I Had A Friend Named Peter*. New York, NY: William Morrow.

Dennison, A., Dennison, A. and Dennison, D. (2005) *After You Lose Someone You Love*. Minneapolis, MN: Free Spirit Publishing.

dePaola, T. (2000) *Nana Upstairs and Nana Downstairs*. New York, NY: Penguin.

Ferguson, D. (1992) *A Bunch of Balloons*. Omaha, NE: Centering Corporation.

Fitzgerald, H. (1992) *The Grieving Child*. New York, NY: Distican.

Fogerty, J. (2000) *Magical Thoughts of Grieving Children*. New York, NY: Baywood Publishing.

Frank, K. (2004) *Good Grief: A Kid's Guide for Dealing With Change and Loss*. Chapin, SC: Youthlight Inc.

Goldman, L. *Children Also Grieve: Talking about Death and Healing*. London, UK: Jessica Kingsley Publishers.

Hogg, E. (2000) *Remembering Honey*. Halifax, Nova Scotia: Nimbus Publishing.

Jones, E. (2001) *Bibliotherapy for Bereaved Children: Healing Reading*. London, UK: Jessica Kingsley Publishers.

LeBlanc, S. (1999) *A Dragon in Your Heart*. London, UK: Jessica Kingsley Publishers.

Nobisso, J. (2000) *Grandma's Scrapbook*. Hong Kong: Regent Publishing Services.

Mellonie, B. and Ingpen, R. (1984) *Lifetimes: A Beautiful Way to Explain Life and Death to Children*. New York, NY: Bantam Books.

Moser, A. (1995) *Don't Despair on Thursdays!: The Children's Grief-Management Book.* Kansas City, KS: Landmark Editions.

Munsch, R. (1996) *Love You Forever.* Toronto, ON: Firefly Books.

Romain, T. (1999) *What on Earth Do You Do When Someone Dies?* Minneapolis, MN: Free Spirit Publishing.

Rothman, J. (2001) *A Birthday Present for Daniel: A Child's Story of Loss.* New York, NY: Prometheus Publishers.

Silverman, J. (1999) *Help Me Say Goodbye.* Minneapolis, MN: Fairview Press.

Smith, W. (2007) *Grandad's Ashes.* London, UK: Jessica Kingsley Publishers.

Turner, M. (2006) *Talking with Children and Young People about Death and Dying.* 2nd edn. London, UK: Jessica Kingsley Publishers.

Varley, S. (1984) *Badgers Parting Gifts.* New York, NY: Lothrop, Lee & Shephard Books.

# Appendix E – Handouts

# Handout 1 – Children's common reactions to traumatic stress

Below are some common reactions that children and adolescents may display after being exposed to trauma.

## Young children (1–6 years)

- Helplessness and passivity; lack of usual responsiveness.

- Generalized fear.

- Heightened arousal and confusion.

- Cognitive confusion.

- Difficulty talking about event; lack of verbalization.

- Difficulty identifying feelings.

- Nightmares and other sleep disturbances.

- Separation fears and clinging to caregivers.

- Regressive symptoms (e.g. bedwetting, loss of acquired speech and motor skills).

- Inability to understand death as permanent.

- Anxieties about death.

- Grief related to abandonment by caregiver.

- Somatic symptoms (e.g. stomach aches, headaches).

- Startle response to loud or unusual noises.

- "Freezing" (sudden immobility of body).

- Fussiness, uncharacteristic crying, and neediness.

- Avoidance of or alarm response to specific trauma-related reminders involving sights and physical sensations.

## School-aged children (6–11 years)

- Feelings of responsibility and guilt.

- Repetitious traumatic play and retelling.

- Feeling disturbed by reminders of the event.

- Nightmares and other sleep disturbances.

- Concerns about safety and preoccupation with danger.

- Aggressive behavior and angry outbursts.

- Fear of feelings and trauma reactions.

- Close attention to parents' anxieties.

- School avoidance.

- Worry and concern for others.

- Changes in behavior, mood, and personality.

- Somatic symptoms (complaints about bodily aches and pains).

- Obvious anxiety and fearfulness.

- Withdrawal.

- Specific trauma-related fears; general fearfulness.

- Regression (behaving like a younger child).

- Separation anxiety.

- Loss of interest in activities.

- Confusion and inadequate understanding of traumatic events (more evident in play than in discussion).

- Unclear understanding of death and the causes of "bad" events.

- Giving magical explanations to fill in gaps in understanding.

- Loss of ability to concentrate at school, with lowering of performance.

- "Spacey" or distractible behavior.

# What can parents do?

## Young children (0–2½ years)

- Maintain child's routines around sleeping and eating.

- Avoid unnecessary separations from important caretakers.

- Provide additional soothing activities.

- Maintain calm atmosphere in child's presence.

- Avoid exposing child to reminders of trauma.

- Expect child's temporary regression; don't panic.

- Help a verbal child to give simple names to big feelings; talk about event in simple terms during brief chats.

- Give simple play props related to the actual trauma to a child who is trying to play out the frightening situation (e.g. a doctor's kit, a toy ambulance).

## Young children (2½–6 years)

- Listen to and tolerate child's retelling of the event.

- Respect child's fears; give child time to cope with fears.

- Protect child from re-exposure to frightening situations and reminders of trauma, including scary TV programs, movies, stories, and physical or locational reminders of trauma.

- Accept and help the child to name strong feelings during brief conversations (the child cannot talk about these feelings or the experience for long).

- Expect and understand child's regression while maintaining basic household rules.

- Expect some difficult or uncharacteristic behavior.

- Set firm limits on hurtful or scary play and behavior.

- If child is fearful, avoid unnecessary separations from important caretakers.

- Maintain household and family routines that comfort child.

- Avoid introducing experiences that are new and challenging for child.

- Provide additional night-time comforts when possible such as night-lights, stuffed animals, and physical comfort after nightmares.

- Explain to child that nightmares come from the fears a child has inside, that they aren't real, and that they will occur less frequently over time.

- Provide opportunities and props for trauma-related play.

- Try to discover what triggers sudden fearfulness or regression.

- Monitor child's coping in school and daycare by expressing concerns and communicating with teaching staff.

## School-aged children (6–11 years)

- Listen to and tolerate child's retelling of the event.

- Respect child's fears; give child time to cope with fears.

- Increase monitoring and awareness of child's play which may involve secretive re-enactments of trauma with peers and siblings; set limits on scary or hurtful play.

- Permit child to try out new ways of coping with fearfulness at bedtime: extra reading time, leaving the radio on, or listening to a tape in the middle of the night to erase the residue of fear from a nightmare.

- Reassure the older child that feelings of fear and behaviors that feel out of control or babyish (e.g. bedwetting) are normal after a frightening experience and that he or she will feel better with time.

# Handout 2 – Signs of serious problems with grief and loss

Children who are having serious problems with *grief* and *loss* may show one or more of these signs:

- An extended period of depression in which the child loses interest in daily activities and events.

- Inability to sleep, loss of appetite, prolonged fear of being alone.

- Acting much younger for an extended period.

- Excessively imitating the dead person.

- Repeated statements of wanting to join the dead person.

- Withdrawal from friends.

- Sharp drop in school performance or refusal to attend school.

If these signs persist, professional help may be needed.

# Handout 3 – Symptoms and behaviors associated with depression in children

- Crying, feeling sad, helpless, or hopeless.

- Feeling discouraged or worthless.

- Loss of interest or pleasure in others or most activities.

- Fatigue and loss of energy nearly every day.

- Bad temper, irritable, easily annoyed.

- Fearful, tense, anxious.

- Repeated rejection by other children.

- Drop in school performance.

- Inability to sit still, fidgeting, or pacing.

- Repeated emotional outbursts, shouting, or complaining.

- Doesn't talk to other children.

- Repeated physical complaints without medical cause (headaches, stomach aches, aching arms or legs).

- Significant increase or decrease in appetite (not due to appropriate dieting).

- Change in sleep habits.

## Serious and critical symptoms of depression in children

- Suicidal thoughts, feelings or self-harming behavior.

- Abuse or prolonged use of alcohol or other drugs.

- Symptoms of depression combined with strange or unusual behavior.

# Handout 4

## *How teachers can help children deal with grief and loss*

- Acknowledge the loss quickly and provide an environment in which children feel safe to share.

- Prepare children in the class for the return of a child who has been absent due to a loss. Discuss with children what to say, and what not to say.

- Ask the children to participate in a group letter of support to the child.

- Provide learning activities in the curriculum by discussing death, loss, bereavement in current events. Use feeling words and grief words in everyday conversations.

- Discuss different cultural and religious differences in death rituals and funerals.

# Appendix F

# Group screening questionnaire

**Directions** Facilitator will need to ask and score the questions with the child:

Name: _ _ _ _ _ _ _ _ _ _ _ _ _ _ _ Age: _ _ _ _ _ _ _ _ _ _ _ _ _ _ _

Grade: _ _ _ _ _ _ _ _ _ _ _ _ _ _ _ _ _ _ _ _ Date: _ _ _ _ _ _ _ _ _

I was _ _ _ _ _ _ _ years old when I experienced the loss of someone

meaningful to me.

This person was a _ _ _ _ _ _ _ _ _ parent _ _ _ _ _ _ _ _ _ friend _ _ _

brother _ _ _ _ _ _ _ _ sister _ _ _ _ _ _ _ _ _ other _ _ _ _ _ _ _ _ _

This loss occurred as a result of a _ _ _ _ _ _ _ _ death _ _ _ _ _ _ _ _ _

accident _ _ _ _ _ _ _ illness _ _ _ _ _ _ _ _ suicide _ _ _ _ _ _ divorce

_ _ _ _ _ _ _ _ _ separation _ _ _ _ _ _ _ _ moving _ _ _ _ _ _ _ _ _

new school _ _ _ _ _ _ _ _ _ _ _ _ family conflict _ _ _ _ _ _ _ _ pet loss

_ _ _ _ _ _ _ _ _ _ _ toy loss _ _ _ _ _ _ _ _ _ other _ _ _ _ _ _ _ _ _

Who has helped you get over this loss the most? _ _ _ _ _ _ mother _ _ _

father _ _ _ _ _ _ _ _ sister _ _ _ _ _ _ _ _ brother _ _ _ _ _ _ _ other

family _ _ _ _ _ _ _ _ friend _ _ _ _ _ _ _ _ _ other _ _ _ _ _ _ _ _ _

When the loss happened, what were some of the feelings you felt? _ _ _ _ _

anger _ _ _ _ _ _ feeling left _ _ _ _ _ _ _ confusion _ _ _ _ _ _ anxiety

_ _ _ _ _ _ fear _ _ _ _ _ _ _ _ sadness _ _ _ _ _ _ _ _ guilt _ _ _

disbelief _ _ _ _ _ _ _ shock _ _ _ _ _ _ _ _ _ relief _ _ _ _ _ _ _ peace

_ _ _ _ _ other

Did you feel alone and that no one understood? _ _ _ _ _ _ _ _ _ _ _ _ _ _

Did you have worries about your own death? _ _ _ _ _ _ _ _ _ _ _ _ _ _

Did you feel support from your family and friends? _ _ _ _ _ _ _ _ _ _ _ _

Did you have problems concentrating at school sometimes? _ _ _ _ _ _ _ _

What helped you to feel better? _ _ _ _ _ _ _ _ _ _ _ _ _ _ _ _ _ _ _ _ _ _

Would you like to attend a group where other children have also had a loss? _

_ _ _ _ _ _ _ _ _ _ _ _ _ _ _ _ _ _ _ _ _ _ _ _ _ _ _ _ _ _ _ _ _ _ _ _ _ _

What would be helpful to you to get through this loss? _ _ _ _ _ _ _ _ _ _ _

_ _ _ _ _ _ _ _ _ _ _ _ _ _ _ _ _ _ _ _ _ _ _ _ _ _ _ _ _ _ _ _ _ _ _ _ _ _

# Group evaluation activity

## ACTIVITY 14 NEW PERSPECTIVES

## A new way to remember and feel

Write or draw below about how you are *feeling now* or what feeling words you have since you have worked through these exercises: _____

_____

_____

_____

_____

_____

Write about or draw how you are feeling about your goodbye time now: _____

_____

_____

_____

_____

_____

## Space to draw how you are feeling now:

# About the author

Julia Sorensen works in private practice with individuals and families in North America.

Julia holds a Masters degree in psychology and is studying towards a doctorate in psychology. Julia is a registered professional counselor and holds specialist certifications in Cognitive Behavioral Therapy and Cognitive Behavioral School Counseling.

Julia has written articles on such topics as grief, bullying, and parenting for community, educational, and parenting groups. She may be reached at:

Email: julia@thecbtcoach.com

Website: www.thecbtcoach.com

Website: http://grieftopeace.com